JEROME KERN
THE MAN AND HIS MUSIC
IN STORY, PICTURE AND SONG

Produced and Written by Hugh Fordin,

author of "THE WORLD OF ENTERTAINMENT!
Hollywood's Greatest Musicals; The
Freed Unit at MGM" published by
Doubleday & Company, Inc.

Book Project Director: Joseph Abend
Music Arranged and Edited by Dan Fox
Art Direction: Mel Rogers
Research and Editing: Margaret McGovern

Published by T. B. Harms Company
Santa Monica, California
Library of Congress Catalogue Card No. 74-29146

Exclusive Music Trade Distributor
Cimino Publications Incorporated

Exclusive Book Trade Distributor
Harper & Row, Publishers, Inc.

TABLE OF CONTENTS

Grateful Acknowledgements are made for the following:

Photographs

Betty Kern Miller, the Arthur Freed Archives, American
Society of Composers, Authors and Publishers, MGM Studios,
Twentieth Century Fox, Inc., Columbia Pictures, RKO Pictures,
a division of RKO General, Inc. and Culver Pictures, Inc.

Excerpts and Quotations

Hugh Fordin for excerpts from "Oscar Hammerstein II,
Getting To Know Him," Copyright © 1975 by Hugh Fordin
to be published by Random House, Inc.; Edna Ferber,
"A Peculiar Treasure," Copyright © 1938, 1939 by
Edna Ferber; Copyright © 1960 by Morris L. Ernst, et al.,
Trustees; Copyright © Renewed 1966 by Edna Ferber; Fred
Astaire for excerpts from his autobiography, "Steps In Time;"
Ira Gershwin for quotations from his book, "Lyrics On
Several Occasions;" excerpts from Oscar Hammerstein II's
"The Jerome Kern Song Book," Copyright © 1955 by Simon and
Schuster, Inc. and Dorothy Blanchard Hammerstein for
use of unpublished lyric by Oscar Hammerstein II and
the eulogy written and delivered by Oscar Hammerstein II
at the funeral of Jerome Kern.

Cover

Hirschfeld Drawing loaned by Betty Kern Miller.

JEROME KERN: THE MAN AND HIS MUSIC

WITH HIS WIFE, EVA

Jerome David Kern was born in New York City on January 28, 1885. This date seems significant in the light of the statement above—Kern was born a generation after Victor Herbert and a generation before Richard Rodgers. Factually as well as stylistically, he was the bridge between the old "Viennese" school and the new indigenous "American" one.

His first published song, "At the Casino" was written while he was attending Newark High School in New Jersey. After high school he studied piano, harmony and composition at the New York College of Music and at Heidelburg's famous Conservatory in Germany.

In 1905 he returned home and went to work for T. B. Harms & Co., music publishers. He wanted practical experience and knowledge of the publishing business as well as a chance to make contacts and perhaps work his way closer to his goal: writing for the theater. He became the company's utility man, office boy, piano player and general jack-of-all-jobs. He worked further as a song-plugger at John Wanamaker's department store; when customers wanted to buy sheet music there, he would play tunes for them, like any salesman demonstrating his product.

Kern's first entry into show business came when he was sent to Hammerstein's Victoria Theatre on 42nd Street, in answer to a hurry call for an accompanist by Marie Dressler, then one of vaudeville's leading knock-about comediennes.

But he was more interested in plugging Kern tunes and he soon found out the best way to do it. Oscar Hammerstein II tells us:

He became a rehearsal pianist, and he used this job as a device for selling his own compositions. Here is how it would work: about the third week in rehearsals, when the director, producers and the whole company were pretty tired of the Viennese score they had been rehearsing all that time, Jerry would come back early after lunch and start to tinkle a little tune of his own on the piano. Everyone who came in would say, 'What's that?' 'Oh, just a little thing of my own,' Jerry would answer. Pretty soon everyone thought he had discovered a great potential hit. Jerry's tune had a freshness for them that the over-rehearsed score couldn't possibly have, and the first thing you knew he had interpolated a song into the foreign score!

Kern got songs interpolated into shows with such unlikely titles as MR. WIX OF WICKHAM AND THE RICH MR. HOGGENHEIMER. The songs themselves had pretty unlikely titles, too: "Poker Love," for example, and "Don't You Want a Paper, Dearie?" His first hit was "How'd You Like to Spoon With Me?" from a show called THE EARL AND THE GIRL. That song, incidentally is the first in this collection, written in 1905; Kern was twenty.

For the next ten years, his interpolations were taken thicker and faster, through a welter of oddly-named shows: FASCINATING FLORA, MORALS OF MARCUS, MIND THE PAINT GIRL and A WINSOME WIDOW, to name a few. The "interpolation" part of Kern's career was climaxed in 1914 when he wrote one of his loveliest ballads for Julia Sanderson in THE GIRL FROM UTAH: 'They Didn't Believe Me."

**WORKING WITH OTTO HARBACH AT
WARNER BROTHERS, 1930**

In 1915 Kern formed a collaboration with Guy Bolton and P. G. Wodehouse. Together, the three men turned out a series of musicals often referred to as "The Princess Theatre Shows," the Princess Theatre being where most of them were produced. This was a tiny house—capacity two hundred and fifty—on West Thirty-ninth Street. The Princess Theatre shows had much the same invigorating effect on musical theatre that "The Garrick Gaieties" had nine years later. Both were fresh and even startlingly new in sound and form—and both for the same reason: necessity. As Hammerstein describes The Princess Theatre:

There was no room on the stage for large choruses, and so there were no choruses at all except for ensemble quartets and sextets. A revolutionary orchestra was devised by Kern and his orchestrator, Frank Sadler. A new instrumentation called for eleven musicians because that was about all the pit would hold. These small shows had an intimate quality and a finesse that could not be matched in the larger houses on Broadway, and for many years the three collaborators were the darlings of the critics as well as the Broadway audiences they strove to please.

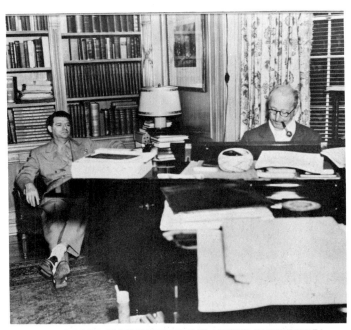

WITH OSCAR HAMMERSTEIN II AT HIS CALIFORNIA HOME, 1938

Kern's career was now under full steam. In 1915 he was represented in seven productions on Broadway—three of them complete scores. In 1917 and 1918 there were five Kern musicals. One of them, LEAVE IT TO JANE, took him only eight days to write. And not only did the titles of his shows be-

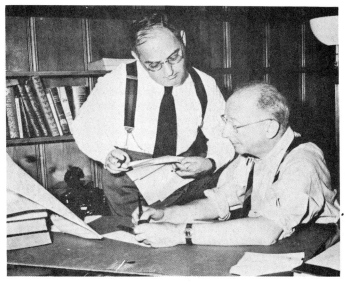

WORKING WITH IRA GERSHWIN ON "COVER GIRL"

come less and less outlandish but the titles of his songs were more familiar. The top of his Broadway career was reached in 1927 with the production of SHOW BOAT. I say "top" because although he wrote four successful Broadway shows afterwards SHOW BOAT is generally considered Kern's best and most popular score. It is the only Broadway score, to my knowledge, to contain as many as five standards: "Bill," "Can't Help Lovin' Dat Man," "Make Believe," "Why Do I Love You?," and "Ol' Man River." (This list excludes "You Are Love," which is only sightly less well known than the others.)

After ROBERTA in 1933, Kern wrote mostly for motion pictures. His last show was VERY WARM FOR MAY in 1939. It was a flop, though "All The Things You Are," the first act ballad, will still be around when many of today's hit shows are long forgotten.

WITH DOROTHY FIELDS AND GEORGE GERSHWIN

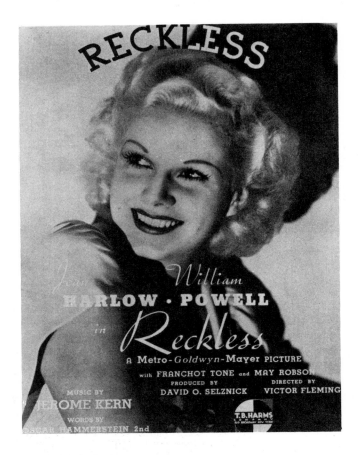

In the course of his career, Kern worked with almost sixty collaborators. The lyricists who worked with him most consistently were P. G. Wodehouse, Otto Harbach, Dorothy Fields and Oscar Hammerstein II. According to the latter, Kern was a sharp-tongued, quick-humored man who demanded almost as much from others as from himself. "He could be reasonably tolerant of incompetence, but he could not stand incompetence masquerading as genius," Hammerstein says. "When he met cheapness of any kind he was merciless and shattering."

Vocal affectations also distressed him. Once he was directing an actress who stressed her R's so outrageously that Kern could bear it no longer. When the actress drawled, in her stagy accent, "Tell me, Mr. Kern—you want me to c-r-r-ross the stage, but I'm behind the table. How shall I get ac-r-r-ross?" Kern, gazing at her like an amiable macaw, countered: "Why, my dear, just r-r-roll over your R's!"

In 1945, Kern came East from California not only to attend rehearsals of a revival of SHOW BOAT but also in connection with the score he was about to write, ANNIE OAKLEY, marking his return to Broadway. A few days after his arrival, he collapsed on Park Avenue and was taken to the Welfare Island hospital where he remained in a state of unconsciousness. Hammerstein's description of this is very moving:

He lay unconscious, in the same institution in which Stephen Foster had died. The critical nature of Jerry's condition did not permit his removal to a private hospital. [Kern was moved two days later]. He was in a ward with some fifty or sixty other patients—mental cases, drunks and derelicts for the most part. The doctors had gathered this heterogeneous group together and explained to them slowly and clearly who the new patient was, and asked them to be very quiet and not create the usual disturbances that characterized this room. Not one man disobeyed. The nurse in charge did not go home that night. She extended her duty for that day to twenty-four hours. When Mrs. Kern expressed her gratitude, the nurse answered simply that he had given so much pleasure to her and to the world that she thought she would like to give something to him. It was clear to us all that special consideration and loving care were being granted to this man in a public hospital not because he was wealthy or powerful but because he had devoted almost all his lifetime to giving the world something it needs and knows it needs—beauty.

Jerome Kern died at 1:10 P.M. on November 11, 1945 of a cerebral thrombosis at Doctors Hospital, East End Avenue and Eighty-eighth Street. He was sixty years old.

The songs in this book, selected from over 1,000 songs and 108 complete scores, are divided into two sections: JEROME KERN ON BROADWAY and JEROME KERN IN HOLLYWOOD. They are all in chronological order.

THE LAST KNOWN PICTURE OF KERN. LEFT TO RIGHT, KAY THOMPSON, ROBERT ALTON, LENNIE HAYTON, LUCILLE BREMER, ARTHUR FREED AND KERN.

THE EARL AND THE GIRL. A musical comedy with book by Seymour Hicks, lyrics by Percy Greenbank and music by Ivan Caryll. "How'd You Like To Spoon With Me" lyrics by Edward Laska and music by Jerome David Kern. Produced by Messrs. Shubert at the Casino Theatre on October 27, 1905. 198 Performances. Cast included Eddie Foy, Georgia Caine and Victor Morely.

ANGELA LANSBURY SINGING "HOW'D YOU LIKE TO SPOON WITH ME?" IN THE 1946 FILMUSICAL "TILL THE CLOUDS ROLL BY."

Edward Laska reminisces about his collaboration with Kern on his first song hit, in 1905, when the composer was twenty:

I used to hang out at the T. B. Harms offices, and I became acquainted with a chap there who was aspiring to become a composer and he asked me to toss him a lyric sometime . . . One day while I was walking there I conceived a sort of burlesque love song centered around the word SPOON. *Reaching the office, I discovered my young friend as usual at the piano and, as usual playing melody after melody into the atmosphere and never bothering to write them down.*

"Get this, Jerry," I said — his full name was Jerome David Kern but he dropped the David right after this song's publication [he did continue to use his middle initial] — get this." I gave him the title line and a rough rhythm. At once, as though it were an old song he knew, he played a chorus in the exact length of time it takes to play the chorus now — and it was corking. "Swell," I said. "Now shoot me a verse." And again, the same thing happened!

"How'd You Like To Spoon With Me?" became a "swinging sensation" as the advertisements of the time referred to it. Six girls singing on flower-decorated swings floated from the stage into the audiences of New York's Casino Theatre, and later, in London's Gaiety.

Laska adds an interesting anecdote that was contained in a letter he once received from Jerome Kern's wife, Eva Leale: "She told me how she met Jerry when she was seventeen, and when he mentioned that he had composed 'How'd You Like To Spoon With Me?' she thought he was jesting, for since her childhood she had known it and always thought it was an old English song . . . Sweetly, she added that the little song had been a great part of the beginning of their thirty-five-year romance."

HOW'D YOU LIKE TO SPOON WITH ME?

words—Edward Laska
music—Jerome Kern

Moderately

(She) I
(He) Well

don't know why I am so ver-y shy, I al-ways was de
I should say I'd spoon with you all day, You fas-ci-nate me

mure, I nev-er knew what sil-ly lov-ers do, No
so, You are so cute you real-ly are a beaut, Through

flirt - ing I'd en - dure; In all my life I've
life with you I'd go. If we were wed our

nev - er kissed a man, I've nev - er winked my eye. But
mar - ried life would be one stead - y hon - ey - moon. From

now at last I'm going to break the ice So how'd you like to
six A. M. 'til twelve o' - clock at night Why all we'd do is

try? _____ So how'd you like to spoon with
spoon. _____ (She) How'd you like to spoon with me? (He) I'd like to

How'd you like to spoon with me?(He) Well rather (She) Sit be-neath an oak tree

large and shad - y, Call me lit - tle toot - sy woot - sy ba - by,

How'd you like to hug and squeeze?(He)Indeed I would Dan - gle me up-on your knees. (He)Oh if could
(She)

(Both)How'd you like to be my lov - ey dov - ey How'd you like to spoon with me.

THE GIRL FROM UTAH. A musical comedy with book and lyrics by James F. Tanner. Music by Paul Ruben and Sidney Jones. Additional songs by Jerome D. Kern. Presented by Charles Frohman at the Knickerbocker Theatre on August 24, 1914. 120 Performances.

Shortly after Kern had completed his songs for this show his publisher, Max Dreyfus, had him play them for Victor Herbert at the Harms offices. "Max," Herbert spouted after Kern finished, "someday this young man will inherit my mantle!"

JULIA SANDERSON AND DONALD BRIAN IN "THE GIRL FROM UTAH."

"They Didn't Believe Me" is Kern's first standard and a song that refuses to date because — apart from the easy, fluid melody — the form is still fresh.

The lyric credit is curious — Herbert Reynolds' name as Kern's collaborator appears on this song for the first time. And yet, the ASCAP records indicate that Reynolds and Michael E. (M. E.) Rourke were one and the same person. In any event, Rourke/Reynolds collaborated on many of Kern's songs during the years 1906-1916.

THEY DIDN'T BELIEVE ME

words—Herbert Reynolds
music—Jerome Kern

So I've got to run a - round ___ Tell - ing peo - ple what I've
And you kissed me where I stood ___ Just like an - y fel - low

Burthen:

found. ___ (He) And when I told them ___
would. ___ (She) And when I told them ___
smoothly

___ how beau - ti - ful you are ___ They did - n't be -
___ how won - der - ful you are ___ They did - n't be -

lieve me ___ They did - n't be - lieve me! ___
lieve me ___ They did - n't be - lieve me! ___

man whose wife one day you'll be
girl whose boy one day you'll be

____ They'll nev-er be - lieve me, ____ They'll nev-er be - lieve me
____ They'll nev-er be - lieve me, ____ They'll nev-er be - lieve me

____ That from this great big world you've cho - sen
____ That from this great big world you've cho - sen

me! 2. (She) Don't know how it hap-pened me!

OH BOY! A musical comedy with books and lyrics by Guy Bolton and P. G. Wodehouse. Presented by William Elliott and F. Ray Comstock at The Princess Theatre on February 20, 1917. 463 Performances. Staged by Edward Royce. Cast included Tom Powers, Anna Wheaton, Edna Mae Oliver and Marion Davies.

From the point of view of output, the year 1917 was a fabulous one for Jerome Kern. January 11th marked the opening of his HAVE A HEART at the Liberty Theatre, and just four nights later on Jan-uary 15th, another Kern show, LOVE O' MIKE had its first performance at the Shubert. On February 20th, after a five week hiatus, OH BOY!, his third and most successful of the Princess Theatre shows, was next, with its popular "Till The Clouds Roll By." Another great hit, LEAVE IT TO JANE, the show that took him eight days to write, came along on August 28th, and the last of the quintet for that year, MISS 1917, opened on November 5th.

JUSTINE JOHNSTONE (LEFT) AND MARION DAVIES IN "OH BOY."

Aside from being one of many Kern standards "Till The Clouds Roll By" also served as the title for his screen biography. The Metro-Goldwyn-Mayer picture also turned out to be the last project Kern had a hand in.

Arthur Freed, the brilliant musical specialist and a close friend of the composer's took charge of producing TILL THE CLOUDS ROLL BY. On September 6, 1945, when principal photography began, Kern was sitting on the side lines in a supervisory capacity.

Satisfied with the proceedings Kern left for New York on November 4th to attend to other business matters. One week later he was dead. When the news reached Freed at the studio he closed down production. Two months later, with an entirely new screenplay, CLOUDS resumed filming.

For the most part, TILL THE CLOUDS ROLL BY was a fictionalized accounting of Kern's career but he would have wanted it that way. During the early script conferences he remarked: "If it tells the truth, it'll be the dullest picture in the world." In any event, the picture stands as a lasting record of Jerome Kern's genius.

TILL THE CLOUDS ROLL BY. An M-G-M (Technicolor) Production based on the life and music of Jerome Kern with Robert Walker as the composer. An all-star cast included Judy Garland, Van Heflin, Lucille Bremer, Dinah Shore, June Allyson, Tony Martin, Kathryn Grayson, Lena Horne, and Frank Sinatra. Featuring Cyd Charisse, Gower Champion, The Wilde Twins, Ray McDonald and Van Johnson. Produced by Arthur Freed. Directed by Richard Whorf. Musical Numbers staged by Robert Alton. Musical Director Lennie Hayton. Orches-trations by Conrad Salinger. Vocal Arrangements by Kay Thompson. Associate Producer Roger Edens.

TILL THE CLOUDS ROLL BY

words—P. G. Wodehouse
music—Jerome Kern

Oh, the rain_____ comes a pit - ter, pat - ter,_____ And I'd

like_____ to be safe in bed._____ Skies are

weep - ing_____ While the world is sleep - ing_____ Trou-ble heap - ing

On our head._____ It is

vain _____ to re - main and chat - ter, _____ And to

wait _____ for a clear - er sky; _____ Hel - ter -

skel - ter _____ I must fly for shel - ter _____ Till the clouds

roll | by. | Oh, the | by. _____

MISS 1917. A revue with book by Guy Bolton, lyrics by P. G. Wodehouse, and additional music by Victor Herbert. Presented by Charles Dillingham and Florenz Ziegfeld at the Century Theatre on November 5, 1917. 48 Performances. Staged by Ned Wayburn. Cast included Lew Fields, Vivienne Segal, Marion Davies, Charles King, Peggy Hopkins [Joyce], Gus Van and Joe Schenck, Irene Castle, Lilyan Tashman, Herbert Fields [Lew Fields' son] George White and Anne Pennington.

Nothing was spared in the way of expense on this star-studded offering. Even the rehearsal pianist was paid $35 a week, which in those days was not too bad. But they got their money's worth, since he happened to be George Gershwin, just turned nineteen, and even then an extraordinarily knowing and alert musician.

During the rehearsal breaks Gershwin would entertain the entire company by playing his own improvisations of the score. This whole experience struck a familiar chord with Kern. It was a variation on the same theme; reminiscent of his own tinkering during the early days. But he was also keenly aware of Gershwin's potential and he brought Max Dreyfus in to listen.

In the years that followed Dreyfus became Gershwin's principal advisor and Kern was merely his idol. In fact he once commented on Kern's influence: "He was the first composer who made me conscious that most popular music was of inferior quality and that musical-comedy music was made of better material."

IRENE CASTLE, THE STAR OF "MISS 1917."

GO LITTLE BOAT

words—P. G. Wodehouse
music—Jerome Kern

Moderately

mp gently

Soft, soft-ly as o-ver the wa-ter we

creep, Winds seem to sigh. Dark, dark is the night and the world is a-

sleep: Wake-ful am I. Slow, slow though the

SALLY. A musical comedy with book by Guy Bolton and P. G. Wodehouse, lyrics by Clifford Grey and B. G. (Buddy) DeSylva, and ballet music by Victor Herbert. Presented by Florenz Ziegfeld at the New Amsterdam Theatre on December 21, 1920. 570 Performances. Staged by Edward Royce. Cast included Marilyn Miller, Walter Catlett and Leon Errol.

With SALLY Kern reverted back to a more traditional kind of musical theatre than The Princess Theatre Shows, a theatre dependant on stars, sets, cast, routines and songs.

As Sally, Marilyn Miller dominated the production. "A Degas figure turned American . . . a Titania of the jazz age," proclaimed the noted critic John Mason Brown. One of the unforgettable moments from the show was her delivery of the touching song "Look For The Silver Lining."

THE MULTI-TALENTED MARILYN MILLER WITH LEON ERROL IN A SCENE FROM "SALLY."

LOOK FOR THE SILVER LINING

words—Bud DeSylva
music—Jerome Kern

JUDY GARLAND IN HER BRILLIANTLY TOUCHING DELIVERY OF "LOOK FOR THE SILVER LINING" FROM "TILL THE CLOUDS ROLL BY." MISS GARLAND PORTRAYED MARILYN MILLER IN THIS FILM.

SUNNY. A musical comedy with book and lyrics by Otto Harbach and Oscar Hammerstein II. Presented by Charles Dillingham at the New Amsterdam Theatre on September 22, 1925. 517 Performances. Staged by Hassard Short. Cast included Marilyn Miller, Paul Frawley, Jack Donahue, Mary Hay and Clifton Webb. [Marilyn Miller's musical numbers staged by Fred Astaire.]

Hammerstein recalls an amusing episode:

Before we went into rehearsal Marilyn Miller returned from Europe and met us in Dillingham's office to listen to the story and score we had written so far. We went through the whole plot and described it, and sang whatever numbers we had written up to that point. She seemed to be listening very attentively. When we were all finished there was a pause, and then Marilyn said, "When do I do my tap specialty?"

THE STAR-STUDDED CAST OF "SUNNY," LEFT TO RIGHT: ESTHER HOWARD, JOSEPH CAWTHORN, DOROTHY FRANCIS, CLIFTON WEBB, MARILYN MILLER, PAUL FRAWLEY, MARY HAY AND JACK DONAHUE.

WHO

words—Otto Harbach
Oscar Hammerstein II
music—Jerome Kern

JUDY GARLAND AND THE MALE ENSEMBLE PERFORMING "WHO" IN KERN'S FILMED LIFE STORY "TILL THE CLOUDS ROLL BY."

SHOW BOAT

THE MUSICAL THAT REVOLUTIONIZED THE AMERICAN THEATER

CHARLES WINNINGER IN A SCENE FROM ORIGINAL FLORENZ ZIEGFELD PRODUCTION OF "SHOW BOAT."

Hammerstein tells how SHOW BOAT first started:

One day Jerry called me up and said, "How would you like to do a show for Ziegfeld? It's got a million dollar title, Show Boat. I said, "Isn't that Edna Ferber's new book?" Jerry said, "Yes. I haven't finished it yet, but I've already bought it from Ferber. Get a copy and read it right away." "Is Ziegfeld enthusiastic?" I asked. "He doesn't know anything about it yet," said Jerry.

SHOW BOAT. A musical comedy with book and lyrics by Oscar Hammerstein II; adapted from Edna Ferber's novel of the same name. Produced by Florenz Ziegfeld at the Ziegfeld Theatre on December 27, 1927. 572 Performances. Dances and ensembles arranged by Sammy Lee. Scenery by Joseph Urban. Dialogue staged by Mr. Hammerstein. Costumes designed by John Harkrider. Musical director Victor Baravalle. Jubilee singers directed by Will Voudry. Cast included Norma Terris, Howard Marsh, Helen Morgan, Charles Winninger, Edna Mae Oliver, Jules Bledsoe, and Aunt Jemima.

PERHAPS THE MOST DRAMATIC PHOTO OF HELEN MORGAN AS SHE SANG "BILL" IN "SHOW BOAT."

Perhaps the most famous of all the Wodehouse-Kern collaboration will remain the delicately shaped torch song "Bill," which was written in 1918 but was dropped from OH, LADY! LADY! Two years later it was used in the Marilyn Miller show SALLY. Again it was dropped. Finally, in a revised version by Hammerstein, it came to rest in SHOW BOAT. When Helen Morgan sang "Bill" she made it sound as though it had been written expressly for her by Kern and Hammerstein. And, although the lyric credit reads P. G. Wodehouse and Oscar Hammerstein II, the latter made it a point of writing:

I am particularly anxious to point out that the lyric for the song "Bill" was written by P. G. Wodehouse. Although he had always been given credit in the program, it has frequently been assumed that since I wrote all the other lyrics for "Show Boat," I also wrote this one, and I have had praise for it which belonged to another man.

BILL

words—P. G. Wodehouse
Oscar Hammerstein II
music —Jerome Kern

THE ROMANTIC TEAM OF LAURA LaPLANTE AND JOSEPH SCHILDKRAUT IN THE FIRST "SHOW BOAT" FILM.

SHOW BOAT. (Original London Production) Produced by Felix Edwardes at the Drury Lane Theatre, London, May 3, 1928.

SHOW BOAT. (Film) Produced by Carl Laemmle Jr. for Universal Pictures. Directed by Harry Pollard. Cast included Laura La Plante, Joseph Schildkraut, Otis Harlan and Emily Fitzroy. Released on May 17, 1929.

"Why Do I Love You?"

Kern had a blind hatred of the word CUPID; it was a favorite word-symbol of operetta lyricists in the Twenties and therefore represented to Kern everything that was corny and old-fashioned in the Viennese school of musical theater. One day while SHOW BOAT was going through its out-of-town tryout Kern gave Hammerstein a tune to set words to. He had worked on it, as he always did, with infinite patience and unbridled enthusiasm and breathlessly awaited the results of Hammerstein's romp with the Muse. Hammerstein, alone in his hotel room, worked out a lyric titled "Why Do I Love You?", but out of some perverse whimsicality also dashed off another lyric on the opposite side of the paper. He handed the latter side to Kern, who snatched at it, propped it on the piano, and started to sing it in his usual wild, impassioned screech. Here is how it began:

CUPID KNOWS THE WAY
by Oscar Hammerstein II

CUPID KNOWS THE WAY; HE'S A NAKED BOY. WHO CAN MAKE YOU SWAY TO LOVE'S OWN JOY. WHEN HE SHOOTS HIS LITTLE ARROW, HE CAN THRILL YOU TO THE MARROW ...

After the initial shock, Kern laughed as heartily as Hammerstein. He also laughed a great deal longer, for he subsequently framed the lyric carefully and displayed it prominently in his home for all visitors to see, the author's name clearly visible. The visitors were not told, however, that it had been written as a joke.

WHY DO I LOVE YOU?

words—Oscar Hammerstein II
music—Jerome Kern

I'm walk - ing on the air, dear,

For life is fair, dear, to

46

MAKE BELIEVE

words—Oscar Hammerstein II
music—Jerome Kern

The game of___ "just sup - pos - ing"___ is the sweet - est ___ game I know,___

Our___ dreams are   more___ ro - man - tic   than the world we   see.

SHOW BOAT (First Revival) Produced by Florenz Ziegfeld at the Casino Theatre on May 19, 1932. 180 Performances. Essentially the same cast as the original production, with the major exceptions of the substitution of Paul Robeson and Dennis King. Including Eva Puck, Sammy White, William Kent, Helen Morgan, and Norma Terris.

SHOW BOAT. (Film—1936) A second screen version with screenplay by Mr. Hammerstein. Produced by Carl Laemmle, Jr. for Universal Pictures. Directed by James Whale. Released on May 14, 1936. Cast included Irene Dunne, Allan Jones, Charles Winninger, Paul Robeson, Helen Morgan, Helen Westley, Donald Cook, Queenie Smith, Sammy White, Hattie McDaniel and Patricia Barry.

well make be - lieve I love you _____ For to

tell the truth _____ I do.

MIRIAM HOPKINS, IRENE DUNNE, HELEN MORGAN, DONALD COOK AND CHARLES WINNINGER FROM THE 1936 SCREEN PRODUCTION OF "SHOW BOAT."

SHOW BOAT. (Revival—1946) A third New York production presented by Mr. Kern and Mr. Hammerstein. Staged by Hassard Short. Directed by Oscar Hammerstein II. Costumes by Lucinda Ballard. Sets Designed by Howard Bay. Musical Director, Edwin MacArthur, Dances by Helen Tamaris. At the Ziegfeld Theatre on January 5, 1946. 418 Performances. Cast included Buddy Ebsen, Carol Bruce, Jan Clayton, Max Showalter, Pearl Primus, Ethel Owen and Charles Fredericks.

SHOW BOAT. (Revival—1948) A fourth New York production presented by Richard Rodgers and Oscar Hammerstein II at The New York City Center on September 7, 1948 with a cast including Carol Bruce, Norwood Smith, Ruth Gates and Billy House.

SHOW BOAT. (Film—1951) A third screen version presented by Metro-Goldwyn-Mayer in Technicolor and released on July 19, 1951. Produced by Arthur Freed. Directed by George Sidney. Musical Numbers Staged by Robert Alton. Associate Producer Roger Edens. Musical Direction by Adolph Deutsch. Orchestrations by Conrad Salinger. Vocal Arrangements by Robert Tucker. Costumes designed Walter Plunkett. Director of Photography Charles Rosher. Art Direction by Jack Martin Smith. Cast included Kathryn Grayson, Ava Gardner, Howard Keel, Joe E. Brown, Marge and Gower Champion, Robert Sterling, Agnes Moorehead, Adele Jergens, Leif Erickson and William Warfield.

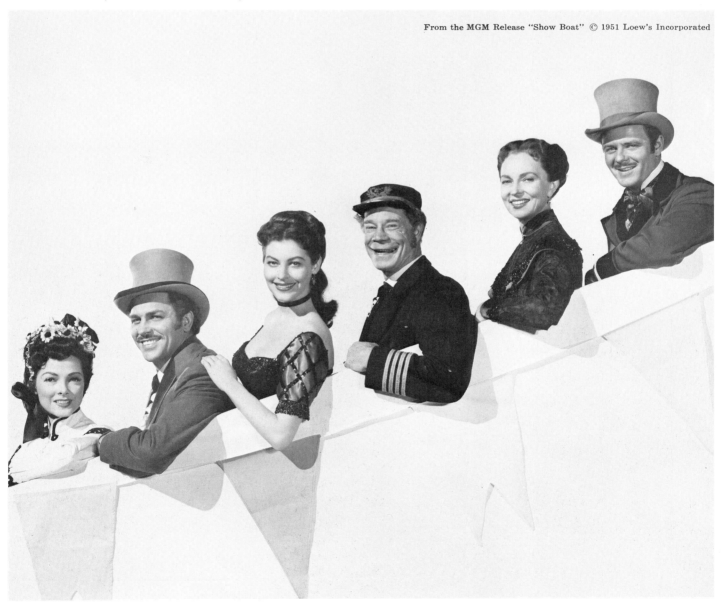

From the MGM Release "Show Boat" © 1951 Loew's Incorporated

MGM'S ALL-STAR "SHOW BOAT" CAST (LEFT TO RIGHT) KATHRYN GRAYSON, HOWARD KEEL, AVA GARDNER, JOE E. BROWN, AGNES MOOREHEAD AND ROBERT STERLING.

YOU ARE LOVE

words—Oscar Hammerstein II
music—Jerome Kern

In her autobiography, A PECULIAR TREASURE, Edna Ferber describes her emotional response when she first heard this song:

As the writing of the musical play proceeded I heard bits and pieces of the score . . . I had heard "Can't Help Lovin' Dat Man" with its love-bemused lyric . . . I had melted under the bewitching strains of "Make Believe" and of "Why Do I Love You?" . . . And then Jerome Kern appeared at my apartment late one afternoon with a strange look of quiet exultation in his eyes. He sat down at the piano. He didn't play the piano particularly well and his singing voice, though true, was negligible. He played and sang "Ol' Man River." The music mounted, mounted, and I give you my word my hair stood on end, the tears came to my eyes, I breathed like a heroine in a melodrama. This was great music. This was music that would outlast Jerome Kern's day and mine. I never have heard it since without that emotional surge.

WILLIAM WARFIELD GIVES HIS MAGNIFICENT RENDITION OF "OL' MAN RIVER" IN THE MGM/ARTHUR FREED 1951 FILM VERSION OF "SHOW BOAT."

OL' MAN RIVER

words—Oscar Hammerstein II
music—Jerome Kern

Slowly, but don't drag

Ol' Man Riv - er, dat Ol' Man Riv - er, He must know sump - in', But don't say noth - in', He jus' keeps roll - in', he keeps on roll - in' a - long. He don't plant 'ta - ters, He

SHOW BOAT. (Revival—1954) A fifth New York production produced by the New York City Opera Company and Light Opera Company. Staged by William Hammerstein. New York City Center on April 8, 1954 (Opera); May 5, 1954 (Light Opera). Opera cast included: Laurel Hurley, Robert Rounseville, Helena Bliss, Marjorie Gateson and Jack Albertson. Light Opera cast included: Burl Ives, Donn Driver, Lawrence Winters and Helen Phillips.

SHOW BOAT. (London Revival—1971) A second London production produced by Harold Fielding at London's Adelphi Theatre on July 29, 1971. Directed and Choreographed by Wendy Toye. Musical Direction and Dance Music Arrangements by Ray Cook. 499 Performances. Cast included Andre Jobin, Cleo Laine, Thomas Carey, Kenneth Nelson and Derek Royle.

LENA HORNE, LEFT, PORTRAYING JULIE, WILLIAM HALLIGAN AS CAPTAIN ANDY, VIRGINIA O'BRIEN AS ELLIE AND BRUCE COWLING AS STEVE IN THE "SHOW BOAT" SCENE FROM THE 1946 MUSICAL "TILL THE CLOUDS ROLL BY."

CAN'T HELP LOVIN' DAT MAN

words—Oscar Hammerstein II
music—Jerome Kern

DON'T EVER LEAVE ME

words—Oscar Hammerstein II
music—Jerome Kern

I'm so de-pen - dent when I need com - fort I al-ways run — to

you. Don't ev - er leave — me 'cause if you do,

I'll have no one — to run to. to.

Over the July 4th weekend in 1929 the Oscar Hammersteins were guests aboard the Kerns' yacht, *the Show Boat,* anchored off New London, Connecticut. Kern played the melody for this song and Hammerstein, quite touched by its beauty, worked out a lyric titled "Don't Ever Leave Me" which he dedicated to his wife, Dorothy, whom he had married two months earlier.

SWEET ADELINE. A musical romance with book and lyrics by Oscar Hammerstein II. Presented by Arthur Hammerstein at the Hammerstein Theatre on September 2, 1929. 234 Performances. Book staged by Reginald Hammerstein. Dances and ensembles staged by Danny Dare. It starred Helen Morgan and featured Charles Butterworth, Irene Franklin and Robert Chisholm.

Helen Morgan, although not actually starred in *Show Boat,* walked away with all the singing and acting honors, and was rewarded by having the next Kern and Hammerstein musical, SWEET ADELINE, written especially for her.

The particular area of popular art that Helen Morgan staked out for herself was a severely limited one, but surely no one has ever done more within a chosen area. Like Ruth Etting and Libby Holman, she was a symbol of a particular type of femininity: mournful, gamely vanquished, singing in a brave little voice about the sadder aspects of love. The well-remembered image of Helen Morgan sitting atop a piano and spinning out her songs with a rare artistry has never faded, and in retrospect it seems odd that her voice was the high, sweet instrument it was, rather than the deeper, more sultry sound that her materials appeared to demand. Nevertheless, she epitomized in many respects the end of an era, those disturbing years of the late Twenties and early Thirties, and left behind her a haunting and tantalizing memory.

HELEN MORGAN AND CHARLES BUTTERWORTH IN A SCENE FROM "SWEET ADELINE" IN WHICH SHE INTRODUCED THE MOVING "WHY WAS I BORN?"

WHY WAS I BORN?

words—Oscar Hammerstein II
music—Jerome Kern

70

SHE DIDN'T SAY YES

words—Otto Harbach
music—Jerome Kern

THE CAT AND THE FIDDLE. A musical comedy with book and lyrics by Otto Harbach. Presented by Max Gordon and the Globe Theatre on October 15, 1931. 395 Performances. Staged by José Ruben. Cast included Odette Myrtil, George Meader, Georges Metaxa and Bettina Hall.

ANOTHER KERN LOVE DUO: JEANETTE McDONALD AND RAMON NAVARRO IN THE FILM VERSION OF "THE CAT AND THE FIDDLE," WHICH INCLUDED THE PRECEDING SONG, "SHE DIDN'T SAY YES" AND "THE NIGHT WAS MADE FOR LOVE."

THE NIGHT WAS MADE FOR LOVE

words—Otto Harbach
music—Jerome Kern

strong, hun-gry arms ___ To lov-ing-ly hold you ___ while two lips on fire: ___

Have ar-dent-ly told you ___ of sweet de - sire. For, like car-ess - ing ___

___ an emp-ty glove Is night with-out some love. ___ The

night was made for love, the night was made for love. ___

MUSIC IN THE AIR. A musical comedy with book and lyrics by Oscar Hammerstein II. Presented by Peggy Fears and A. C. Blumenthall at the Alvin Theatre on November 8, 1932. 342 Performances. Staged by Mr. Hammerstein and Mr. Kern. Cast included Walter Slezak, Katherine Carrington, Tullio Carminati and Al Shean.

"At last the musical drama has been emancipated," proclaimed Brooks Atkinson in his *New York Times* review on the day following the opening of this show. "Jerome Kern and Oscar Hammerstein 2nd have succeeded in telling a romantic story without recourse to the super-anuated formula... What *The Cat and the Fiddle* gallantly began last season Messrs. Kern and Hammerstein have now completed: a fable that flows naturally out of a full-brimming score."

THE HERO AND HEROINE OF "MUSIC IN THE AIR" WALTER SLEZAK AND KATHERINE CARRINGTON AS THEY SANG "I'VE TOLD EV'RY LITTLE STAR" AND "THE SONG IS YOU."

"I've Told Ev'ry Little Star"

"Jerry got the melodic theme from a bird. He swears it!" Hammerstein wrote his colleague Sigmund Romberg. "He heard a finch outside his window singing the first line and he built a refrain on it." Kern and Hammerstein were further indebted to the finch because they opened MUSIC IN THE AIR with this very episode: a composer getting inspiration from a bird song. "Incidentally," Hammerstein added, " 'Ev'ry Little Star' proved to be a stubborn tune and for a whole summer resisted my efforts to set words to it. There were times during those hot August days when I wished the finch had kept his big mouth shut!"

I'VE TOLD EV'RY LITTLE STAR

words—Oscar Hammerstein II
music—Jerome Kern

82

THE SONG IS YOU

words—Oscar Hammerstein II
music—Jerome Kern

I hear mu-sic when I look at you,_____ A beau-ti-ful

theme of ev-'ry dream I ev-er knew._____ Down deep in my

rhap-so-dy of love and youth and spring,_____ The mu-sic is sweet,_____ the words are

true,_____ The song is you.

gradually slowing down

THE STARS OF THE 1934 FOX FILM VERSION OF "MUSIC IN THE AIR," LEFT TO RIGHT, DOUGLAS MONTGOMERY, JUNE LANG, GLORIA SWANSON AND JOHN BOLES.

YESTERDAYS

words—Otto Harbach
music—Jerome Kern

ROBERTA

THE BROADWAY SHOW THAT INTRODUCED THREE GREAT SONGS "THE TOUCH OF YOUR HAND", "YESTERDAYS" AND "SMOKE GETS IN YOUR EYES"

ROBERTA. A musical comedy with book and lyrics by Otto Harbach. Based on Alice Duer Miller's novel *Gowns by Roberta*. "I'll Be Hot to Handle" lyrics by Bernard Dougall. Presented by Max Gordon at the New Amsterdam Theatre on November 18, 1933. 295 Performances. Staged by Hassard Short. Cast included Tamara, Ray Middleton, Bob Hope, Fay Templeton, George Murphy, Sydney Greenstreet and Fred MacMurray.

This was the show that skyrocketed Bob Hope to fame. It was also, by coincidence, the last stage appearance of Fay Templeton, a great Broadway star for over three decades.

"Smoke Gets In Your Eyes"

It took two false starts before this song saw the great light of day. Kern originally had composed it as the signature theme for a radio series but the project collapsed before it went on the air. Again as an instrumental, it was used for a tap routine in SHOW BOAT in front of the show curtain while the scenery was being changed. During the out-of-town tryouts the scene change was eliminated and so was the number. Otto Harbach stumbled across the manuscripts while at work on ROBERTA. "Why not change the tempo," he asked Kern, "if these short notes might be made long notes might it not make an attractive ballad?" Kern agreed, and the end result was "Smoke Gets In Your Eyes."

(The song, thought by most people to be Kern's most well known work, starts on page 98)

FOUR OF THE PRINCIPALS, LEFT TO RIGHT, GEORGE MURPHY, RAY MIDDLETON, TAMARA, AND BOB HOPE.

Of all her husband's compositions this song was Eva Kern's favorite.

THE TOUCH OF YOUR HAND

words—Otto Harbach
music—Jerome Kern

hand in hand___ Through-out a hap - py land___ That we had

planned.___ (He) I had hoped that our

way might end Where the sky and blue hor -

i - zon blend. Yet we've both walked our

G#   A   Bm   G#   A   A9   Bm

sigh - ing for one touch of rain, Then you may

F#m   Em7

bor - row, Some glimpse of my

Bm   G6   Em7

sor - row, And you'll un - der -

D/A   E7/A   A7

stand_____ How I long for the touch of your

mf   *p*

*Voices hold till **

SMOKE GETS IN YOUR EYES

words—Otto Harbach
music—Jerome Kern

VERY WARM FOR MAY. A Musical comedy with book and lyrics by Oscar Hammerstein II. Presented by Max Gordon at the Alvin Theatre on November 17, 1939. 59 Performances. Staged by Vincente Minnelli. Dances staged by Albertina Rasch and Harry Losee. Book directed by Mr. Hammerstein. Cast included Grace McDonald, Jack Whiting, Hiram Sherman and Donald Brian.

TONY MARTIN, WHO HAD ONE OF HIS MOST OUTSTANDING SUCCESSES WITH "ALL THE THINGS YOU ARE" AND THE COMPOSER IN 1939.

"All The Things You Are" was one of the most surprising hits Kern and Hammerstein had. They never thought the public would take to it because the middle of the refrain contains three changes of key.

ALL THE THINGS YOU ARE

words—Oscar Hammerstein II
music—Jerome Kern

The dear-est things I know __ are what you are.

Some day my hap-py arms will hold you, And

some day I'll know that mo-ment di-vine, When

all the things you are, are mine.

KERN IN HOLLYWOOD

ROBERTA. An RKO Picture released in March, 1935. Starred Irene Dunne, Fred Astaire and Ginger Rogers; featured Randolph Scott and Helen Westley. Lyrics by Otto Harbach, Bernard Dougall, Oscar Hammerstein II, Dorothy Fields and Jimmy Mc-Hugh. Produced by Pandro S. Berman. Directed by William A. Seiter.

ROBERTA was the start of Jerome Kern in Hollywood. (His score for the 1931 film THE MAN IN THE SKY cannot be counted because Warner Brothers cut all the songs and released it as MEN OF THE SKY, a straight picture.) This film version of his recent stage success also served to introduce him to a woman who became one of his most important collaborators: Dorothy Fields.

Miss Fields recounted this to me: "It's very curious how I first started working with Jerry. Of course, he knew my father and my brothers [her father was the famous Broadway Actor-Producer, Lew Fields, who was also part of that famous comedy team, Weber and Fields. Her brothers were Herbert and Joseph, both Broadway playwrights]. I was working at RKO and Pan Berman, who was producing ROBERTA, asked me if I'd take a couple of days and work on it. He said, 'we have a seriously uneven melody of Jerome Kern's that he's given us to add to the score; it needs a lyric . . .' So I wrote 'Lovely To Look At,' which absolutely astounded Berman. And he had the nerve to tell Bill Seiter, the director, to go ahead and shoot it — the whole sequence — and Jerry hadn't even okayed the lyric! Well, I don't have to tell you Jerry loved it and from then on — he asked for me."

GINGER ROGERS AND FRED ASTAIRE IN THEIR FIRST KERN MUSICAL TOGETHER.

"I Won't Dance" first appeared in the Kern-Hammerstein London musical THREE SISTERS early in 1934. Later that same year, with the Hammerstein title but an almost totally new lyric by Dorothy Fields and Jimmy McHugh, it served as a brilliant song and dance number for Fred Astaire in the film version of Roberta.

I WON'T DANCE

words—Dorothy Fields
Jimmy McHugh
music—Jerome Kern

LAUGH AND LOVE DUO: RED SKELTON AND ANN MILLER PROVIDE LAUGHTER AS WELL AS ROMANCE IN "LOVELY TO LOOK AT."

From the MGM Release "Lovely To Look At" © 1952 Loew's Incorporated

LOVELY TO LOOK AT. (Second Film Version) An M-G-M Picture (Technicolor) released in December, 1952. An adaptation of Roberta which starred Kathryn Grayson, Red Skelton, Howard Keel, Marge and Gower Champion, and Ann Miller. Produced by Jack Cummings [married to Kern's daughter, Betty, at the time]. Directed by Mervyn LeRoy and Vincente Minnelli.

LOVELY TO LOOK AT

words—Dorothy Fields
Jimmy McHugh
music—Jerome Kern

Optional repeat for alternate verse.

I DREAM TOO MUCH. An RKO Picture released in November, 1935. It starred Lily Pons and featured Henry Fonda, Eric Blore, Osgood Perkins [actor Anthony Perkins' father], Lucille Ball and Micha Auer. Lyrics by Dorothy Fields. Produced by Pandro S. Berman. Directed by John Cromwell.

LILY PONS HAS A HANDSOME ACCOMPANIST IN HENRY FONDA IN THE FILM "I DREAM TOO MUCH."

I DREAM TOO MUCH

words—Dorothy Fields
music—Jerome Kern

120

SWING TIME. An RKO Picture released in August, 1936. It starred Fred Astaire and Ginger Rogers and featured Helen Broderick and Victor Moore. Lyrics by Dorothy Fields. Produced by Pandro S. Berman. Directed by George Stevens.

Arthur Schwartz, the noted composer-producer has an amusing story about Kern and SWING TIME:

Jerry has played the piano for years, but with no particular flair. In fact, what he does to his own tunes at the piano is sheer murder. This is not helped by the fact that he never attempts to "put over" his songs. When he first played the score of SWING TIME for the RKO executives, there was silence. Stony, if not stricken, faces were all over the room. Yet, out of his score for that film came "The Way You Look Tonight," "A Fine Romance" and the bouncy "Pick Yourself Up."

"The Way You Look Tonight" won the Academy Award as the best song of 1936.

GINGER ROGERS, AS SHE LOOKS AT FRED ASTAIRE, WONDERS IF THIS COULD BE "A FINE ROMANCE."

(THIS IS) A FINE ROMANCE

words—Dorothy Fields
music—Jerome Kern

Additional Words

She:
A fine romance,
With no kisses!
A fine romance,
My friend, this is!
We two should be like clams in a dish of chowder;
But we just fizz like parts of a Seidlitz Powder.
A fine romance
With no clinches,
A fine romance
With no pinches.
You're just as hard to land as the "Ile de France!"
I haven't got a chance.
This is a fine romance!

He:
A fine romance
My dear duchess,
Two old fogies
Who need crutches!
True love should have the thrills that a healthy crime has!
We don't have half the thrills that the "March of Time" has!
A fine romance,
My good woman,
My strong "aged in the wood" woman!
You never give the orchids I sent a glance!
No! You like cactus plants,
This is a fine romance.

PICK YOURSELF UP

words—Dorothy Fields
music—Jerome Kern

Moderately, with a lilt

Noth-ing's im-pos-si-ble I have found, for when my chin is on the ground, I pick my-self up, dust my-self off, start all o-ver a-gain. Don't lose your con-fi-dence if you slip, be grate-ful for a pleas-ant trip, And

128

take a deep breath, pick your-self up,

dust your-self off, start all o - ver a - gain.

Interlude:

I'll get some self as - sur-ance if your en - dur-ance is great.

I'll learn by eas - y sta - ges if you're cour - ag-eous and wait.

To feel the strength I want to, I must hang on to your hand,

May - be by the time I'm fif - ty I'll get up and do a nif - ty.

THE WAY YOU LOOK TONIGHT

words—Dorothy Fields
music—Jerome Kern

HELEN BRODERICK AND GINGER ROGERS CONGRATULATE VICTOR MOORE AND FRED ASTAIRE ON
"THE WAY THEY LOOK TONIGHT."

HIGH, WIDE AND HANDSOME. A Paramount Picture released in May, 1937. It starred Irene Dunne and featured Randolph Scott, Dorothy Lamour, Elizabeth Patterson, Akim Tamiroff, Ben Blue, William Frawley and Alan Hale. Original Story, Screenplay and Lyrics by Oscar Hammerstein II. Produced by Arthur Hornblow Jr. Directed by Rouben Mamoulian.

CHARLES BICKFORD, IRENE DUNNE AND RANDOLPH SCOTT IN A DRAMATIC SCENE FROM "HIGH, WIDE AND HANDSOME."

"The Folks Who Live On The Hill"
This is Kern in his loosest, most rhapsodic mood. There is enough melodic material in this piece for three different songs. Hammerstein's lyrics are pure and sentimental. He was always bothered by the obvious rhyme: "Our veranda will command a . ."

THE FOLKS WHO LIVE ON THE HILL

words—Oscar Hammerstein II
music—Jerome Kern

"The folks who live on the hill."

Some - day _____ we may be add - ing a thing or two, ___

A wing or two, ___
(false accent intended)
We will make chang - es as an - y fam' - ly

will, _____ But we will al - ways be called ___

"Can I Forget You?"
This piece, with its naive, folksongish melody is rather like the songs of Stephen Foster.

IRENE DUNNE AND RANDOLPH SCOTT

CAN I FORGET YOU?

words—Oscar Hammerstein II
music—Jerome Kern

Burthen: **Moderato**

JOY OF LIVING. An RKO Picture released in May, 1938. Starred Irene Dunne and featured Douglas Fairbanks Jr., Alice Brady, Guy Kibbe and Lucille Ball. Lyrics by Dorothy Fields. Directed by Tay Garnett.

This film marked the sixth appearance for Irene Dunne in a Kern musical. In 1927 she understudied the role of Magnolia in the Broadway production of SHOW BOAT. When the National Company arrived in Los Angeles, with Miss Dunne now in the leading part, she was grabbed by the Hollywood studios. Her roles in Kern filmusicals were: ROBERTA (1935); SWEET ADELINE (1935); SHOW BOAT (1936); HIGH, WIDE AND HANDSOME (1937); and JOY OF LIVING (1938).

A POSTER FOR "THE JOY OF LIVING" SHOWING LUCILLE BALL IN ONE OF HER EARLIEST ROLES.

When I first heard "You Couldn't Be Cuter" I wouldn't believe that it had been written by Kern. It bears none of his characteristics. But that has no validity if you remember that he also wrote that sexy-vamp, "I'll Be Hot to Handle" for the musical ROBERTA.

As to the lyrics for this song: Dorothy Fields once told me that her son, David, then just an infant, inspired the title.

YOU COULDN'T BE CUTER

words—Dorothy Fields
music—Jerome Kern

got me, lit - tle fel - la, I'm sunk! I'm gone! I'm hooked!

gradually slowing down

Burthen:

Moderately

You could - n't be cut - er___ Plus that you could - n't be smart - er___

mp *lightly with a lilt*

___ Plus that in - tel - li - gent face you have a dis - grace - ful

charm for me. You could - n't be keen - er,___ you look so

149

fresh from the clean - er, _____ You are the lit - tle grand slam I'll

bring to my fam - i - ly. _____ My ma will show you an

al - bum of me that - 'll bore you to tears! _____ And

you'll at - tract all the rel - a-tives we have dodged for years and years. And what - 'll they tell me? Ex - act - ly, what - 'll they tell me?

They'll say you could - n't be nic - er, could - n't be sweet - er,
crescendo to the end

Gmaj7 G6 Am7 D7

Bm7 Em7 Cmaj7 Am7 Bm7 E7–9 Am7 D7

could - n't be bet - ter, could - n't be smooth - er, could - n't be cut - er ba - by than you

1. G D7 2. G F#6 G6

are! _____ You are! _____

ONE NIGHT IN THE TROPICS. A Universal Picture released in December, 1940. Starred Bud Abbott and Lou Costello and featured Allan Jones, Nancy Kelly and Leo Carillo. Lyrics by Dorothy Fields. "Your Dream (Is the Same as My Dream)" lyrics by Otto Harbach and Oscar Hammerstein II (from the stage production of GENTLEMAN UNAFRAID). Directed by A. Edward Sutherland.

ROBERT CUMMINGS, NANCY KELLY (BACK ROW) SEEM TO OBJECT TO PEGGY MORAN'S HEAD ON ALLAN JONES' SHOULDER.

REMIND ME

words—Dorothy Fields
music—Jerome Kern

LADY BE GOOD. A Metro-Goldwyn-Mayer Picture released in May, 1941. Cast included Ann Sothern, Eleanor Powell, Robert Young and Lionel Barrymore. Songs by George and Ira Gershwin, Arthur Freed and Roger Edens, and Jerome Kern and Oscar Hammerstein II. Musical Numbers staged by Busby Berkeley. Musical Director Georgie Stoll. Orchestrations by Conrad Salinger and Leo Arnaud. Associate Producer Roger Edens. Directed by Norman McLeod. Produced by Arthur Freed.

"The Last Time I Saw Paris" was not written for LADY BE GOOD nor any other motion picture or stage play. Messrs. Kern and Hammerstein just allowed Arthur Freed to use it in his filmusical.

Hammerstein tells about how the song came to be written:

This was the only song that I've ever written under any kind of compulsion. The Germans had just taken Paris and I couldn't get my mind on anything else at all. I loved the city very much and I hated the idea of it falling. I thought of the enemy tramping through the streets and taking all the gaiety and beauty out of the hearts of the people there. I thought of Mistinguette and her vastly insured legs and her shock of hair that she would shake when she sang. I thought of Chevalier with his straw hat. And, not just the beauty of the parks or the loveliness in the museums but everything that was Paris: good and bad and of high quality and of cheapness. And this was kind of a lament.

When I called Jerry and asked him to write some music for it, he almost fell dead. In all the years we'd been working together, this was the first time I had completed a lyric that he would have to set to music. He always wrote the melody and then I would fit words to it.

Kern took the words down over the telephone and three days later, when Hammerstein arrived on the coast, he was handed the finished manuscript.

Incidentally, both men were quite upset upon receiving news that "The Last Time I Saw Paris" had won an Academy Award. To be sure, they were pleased that the song was such a success, but, it had not been written for a motion picture. Kern saw to it that the Academy changed its rules making only those songs expressly written for a film eligible for an Oscar.

156

ALL-STAR CAST, RED SKELTON, ELEANOR POWELL, ROBERT YOUNG, AND JOHN CARROLL WITH ANN SOTHERN, WHO INTRODUCED THE ACADEMY-AWARD WINNING SONG IN THIS PICTURE.

THE LAST TIME I SAW PARIS

words—Oscar Hammerstein II
music—Jerome Kern

ev - 'ry street ca - fe. The last time I saw Par - is, Her

trees were dressed for spring, And lov - ers walked be - neath those trees, And

birds found songs to sing. I dodged the same old tax - i - cabs that

a little brighter

I had dodged for years; The cho - rus of their squeak - y horns was

* *G♯ and G♮ together.*

YOU WERE NEVER LOVELIER. A Columbia Picture (Technicolor) released in December, 1942. Starred Fred Astaire and Rita Hayworth and featured Adolphe Menjou. Lyrics by Johnny Mercer. Directed by William A. Seiter.

Fred Astaire, in his autobiography STEPS IN TIME, describes the rehearsals on this film:

Rita and I had a romantic type dance to the song "You Were Never Lovelier." Keeping the laughs going during the intervals was a part of the day's work and I always tried to think up some gag to play on Rita. In one instance I called out, "well — here we go — I'm beginning to like this place — it doesn't get me down anymore, I'm used to it — ready, Rita?"

Up jumped Rita at once and came to me to start our first step together. As I took hold of her two arms she let out one scream and backed away. I had just dipped both my hands and arms in a bucket of ice which we kept for Coca-Cola bottles. That broke up rehearsals for an hour or so.

THE DEBONAIR ADOLPHE MENJOU, THE SULTRY MISS RITA HAYWORTH AND THE FASTEST-FEET IN THE WEST, FRED ASTAIRE.

DEARLY BELOVED

words—Johnny Mercer
music—Jerome Kern

Moderately

Dear - ly be - lov - ed, how clear - ly I see,

8va lower till *

Some - where in heav - en you were fash - ioned for me,

*

An - gel eyes_____ knew you,_____

rush a bit, but more rhapsodically

An - gel voic - es led me to you;_____

hold back

You Were Never Lovelier

words—Johnny Mercer
music—Jerome Kern

Moderately

soft and smooth

I was nev-er a-ble to re-cite a fa-ble that would make the par-ty

Organ pedal tacet till burthen

bright. Sit-ting at the ta-ble I was nev-er a-ble

to be-come the host's de-light. But now you've

giv - en me my af - ter din - ner sto - ry,

I'll just de - scribe you as you are in all your glo - ry.

Burthen:

You were nev - er love - li - er, you were nev - er so

fair; Dreams were nev - er love - li - er, par - don me__ if I

168

stare. Down the sky the moon-beams fly to light your

face, I can on - ly say they chose the prop - er

place. You were nev - er love - li - er,

and to coin a new phrase; I was

I'M OLD FASHIONED

words—Johnny Mercer
music—Jerome Kern

Liltingly

in tempo

I'm old fash-ioned, I love the moon-light, I love the

old fash-ioned things:_____ The sound of rain up-

on a win-dow pane, The star-ry song that A-pril

sings._____ *(no breath!)* This year's fan-cies are pass - ing

172

CAN'T HELP SINGING. A Universal Picture (Technicolor) released in December, 1944. Starred Deanna Durbin and featured Robert Paige, David Bruce and Akim Tamiroff. Lyrics by E. Y. Harburg. Produced by Felix Jackson. Directed by Frank Ryan.

FOR OPENERS, I THINK THE TITLE OF THIS FILM IS MORE DESCRIPTIVE OF DEANNA DURBIN THAN HER VEHICLE. KIDDING ASIDE, KERN WAS ONCE AGAIN AT HOME WITH A PERIOD PIECE: THE FIRST CALIFORNIA SETTLERS.

From the film "Can't Help Singing" Courtesy of Universal Pictures

CAN'T HELP SINGING

words—E. Y. Harburg
music—Jerome Kern

Burthen:

COVER GIRL. A Columbia Picture (Technicolor) released in March, 1944. Starred Rita Hayworth and Gene Kelly and featured Phil Silvers, Lee Bowman, Jinx Falkenburg, Otto Kruger and Eve Arden. Lyrics by Ira Gershwin. Produced by Arthur Schwartz. Directed by Charles Vidor. Musical Director Morris Stoloff. Musical Supervisor Saul Chaplin. Orchestration by Conrad Salinger and Paul Weston.

THE CURBSTONE KIDS: GENE KELLY, RITA HAYWORTH AND PHIL SILVERS DANCING ON A BROOKLYN SIDEWALK.

From the Columbia Picture "Cover Girl" ©D-194-I91

"Sure Thing"

Ira Gershwin, in his book LYRICS ON SEVERAL OCCASIONS, speaks about his work with Kern:

It was in 1939 that Kern was between assignments and I wrote nine or ten songs with him. Nothing ever happened to them although both of us liked several. During this time he played me many other tunes I liked but just didn't get around to. Some four years later, COVER GIRL period, I tried to remind him of a lovely tune of the earlier period by humming a snatch of it. But he had never put it on paper, and couldn't recall it. I told him his daughter Betty had been very fond of this melody, so he called her in and between us and our snatches, it came to him. "Good tune," he said. "What about it?" I told him it had begun haunting me that morning, and if he could split the opening note into two notes, I had a two-word on-the-nose title for the flashback number in the film — one which had a production idea for the choreographer and the designer. When he heard the title, "Sure Thing," with its race-track backgound, [Kern was an avid racing enthusiast] he said: "Of course — nothing to it — in fact, the two notes make a better announcement."

LONG AGO (AND FAR AWAY)

words—Ira Gershwin
music—Jerome Kern

Sure Thing

words—Ira Gershwin
music—Jerome Kern

But, win or lose, what - ev - er comes up, you're thumbs up with

me. One thing I'm sure I'm sure of all my life through

If love can fig - ure out a sure thing, that

sure thing is you.

CORNELL WILDE USES HIS CHARM ON LINDA DARNELL, RIGHT, AS JEANNE CRAIN DISAPPROVES IN "CENTEN-NIAL SUMMER."

CENTENNIAL SUMMER. A Twentieth Century-Fox Film (Technicolor) released in July, 1946. Starred Jeanne Crain, Cornell Wilde, Linda Darnell, William Eythe, Walter Brennan, Constance Bennett and Dorothy Gish. Lyrics by Leo Robin, E. Y. Harburg, Johnny Mercer and Oscar Hammerstein II. Musical Director Alfred Newman. Orchestrations by Conrad Salinger, Edward Powell, Earl Hagen and Maurice DePackh. Produced and Directed by Otto Preminger.

In 1945, Metro-Goldwyn-Mayer released their exciting new musical, MEET ME IN ST. LOUIS, which centered around the famous fair of 1906 in that city. The story also made overtures to the already legendary LIFE WITH FATHER.

As was Twentieth Century-Fox's wont, they promptly announced their forthcoming CENTENNIAL SUMMER dealing with a family in 1876 Philadelphia at the time of the Exposition.

Although this old-fashioned tale was ideally suited for Kern's magical touch, this his 109th and final score, presented problems. The cast was made up of non-singers. Otto Preminger, the film's producer and director was not what you would call an expert when it comes to musical production. But, most of all, Kern had a difficult time with his collaborator Leo Robin. "I was completely in awe of Kern from the minute we got together," says Robin, "and it cramped my style a little bit. He used to call me up every day, bugging me: 'You got anything yet?' I wanted so much to please him and to measure up to his high standard that I don't think I did my best work on that picture."

Kern became increasingly anxious as the weeks progressed until he finally had to call "Yip" Harburg, Johnny Mercer and Oscar Hammerstein 2nd to each do a song. Robin did complete two on his own: "Up With A Lark" and "In Love In Vain."

IN LOVE IN VAIN

words—Leo Robin
music—Jerome Kern

This is Kern's last complete work.

ALL THROUGH THE DAY

words—Oscar Hammerstein II
music—Jerome Kern

For in my fan - cy I sweep a - way light

And keep my im - age of the sky,

Just the way we like it, you and I.

rush ahead

Burthen: **Moderato**

slowing down

All through the

very smoothly

Organ pedal tacet for 8 bars

My Friend....JEROME KERN *
by Oscar Hammerstein II

I have promised myself not to play upon your emotions—or on mine. We, in this chapel, are Jerry's "family." We all know him very well. Each of us knows what the other has lost.

I think he would have liked me to say a few words about him. I think he would not have liked me to offer feeble bromides of consolation—butterfly wings of trite condolence to beat against the solid wall of our grief. He would have known our grief was real, and must be faced.

On the other hand, I think Jerry would have liked me to remind you that today's mourning and last week's vigil will soon recede from our memories, in favor of the bright recollections of him that belong to us.

At the moment, Jerry is playing "out of character." The masque of tragedy was never intended for him. His death yesterday and this reluctant epilogue will soon be refocused into their properly remote place in the picture. This episode will soon seem to us to be nothing more than a fantastic and dream-like intrusion on the gay reality that was Jerry's life.

His gayety is what we will remember most— the times he has made us laugh; the even greater fun of making him laugh. It's a strange adjective to apply to a man, but you'll understand what I mean: Jerry was "cute." He was alert and alive. He "bounced." He stimulated everyone. He annoyed some. never bored anyone at any time. There was a sharp edge to everything he thought or said.

...We all know in our hearts that these few minutes we devote to him now are small drops in the ocean of our affections. Our real tribute will be paid over many years of remembering, of telling good stories about him, and thinking about him when we are by ourselves.

We, in this chapel, will cherish our special knowledge of this world figure. We will remember a jaunty, happy man whose sixty years were crowded with success and fun and love. Let us thank whatever God we believe in that we shared some part of the good, bright life Jerry led on this earth.

*(Eulogy delivered by Mr. Hammerstein at the funeral services)